The Introduction of
Sarah Collins Rudolph

The story of the fifth little girl who survived the 16th Street Baptist Church bombing.

Written by LaVon Stennis Williams
with Sarah Collins Rudolph
and George C. Rudolph

OMAHA, NEBRASKA

Text and illustrations ©2021 LaVon Stennis Williams. All Rights Reserved. No part of this publication may be reproduced, stored in a retrieval system, or transmitted in any form or by any means—electronic, mechanical, photocopy, recording, or any other—except for brief quotations in printed reviews, without the prior permission from the publisher.

www.TwoBeePublishing.com

Paperback ISBN: 978-1-7322440-7-8
Hardcover ISBN: 978-1-7322440-8-5

Library of Congress Cataloging Number and Cataloging in Publication Data on file with the publisher.

Illustrated by Rana Digi Paint
http://instagram.com/ranadigipaint

Design and Production by Concierge Marketing Inc.

Printed in the United States of America
10 9 8 7 6 5 4 3 2

Contents

Chapter 1 1

Chapter 2 9

Chapter 3 11

Chapter 4 15

Chapter 5 23

Chapter 6 26

Chapter 7 30

This book is dedicated to the memory of my sister Addie Mae Mae Collins, Denise McNair, Cynthia Wesley Carole Robertson, Virgil Ware and Johnny Robinson and all the children of the Civil Rights Movement—may we always be remembered.

Sarah Collins Rudolph

To all the members of the armed services, especially those of us who served in Vietnam, where we were forced to fight two wars at one time—one abroad and the other at home. Thank you for your service.

George C. Rudolph

To my grandchildren Aniya, Ryleigh, Maxwell, Brandon and Roman, my nieces and nephews and all children reading this book, the sacrifices were made so you can be who you choose to become.

> May you never forget:
> Because of them, you can.

LaVon Stennis Williams (G-von)

Chapter 1

Introducing Sarah Collins Rudolph

Aniya was now trying on her third bow-tie. At the beginning of the school year, she had decided bow-ties would be her signature look; but today was special, and not just any bow-tie would do. Aniya had been selected among all of the 7th graders to introduce the school's Black History Month speaker. Today had to be a special bow-tie. As she was taking off the bow-tie to pick another one, the phone rang. It was her cousin Ryleigh who lived in Mississippi.

"Aniya, it's me."

"Yes, Ryleigh, what is it this time?"

Ryleigh had called Aniya almost every day since learning Aniya would be introducing the speaker. "I almost forgot. Make sure you charge your phone, so your battery doesn't die, and…"

Just as Ryleigh was about to add to her list of things, Aniya interrupted, "Ryleigh, I got it, along with the 50 million other things you want me to do."

"Oh, I know Aniya, but this is very important. I'm so excited. I wish I were there. G-von gave us a book about the girls last Christmas, but it did not mention her. Now you get to meet her. I am so jealous. I…"

"Ryleigh, if you don't get off the phone, I'm never going to make it to school," Aniya said, interrupting Ryleigh again.

Ryleigh quickly blurted out, "And remember it's Sarah with h and Mae with an e."

"Goodbye, Ryleigh."

Ever since Ryleigh learned Aniya would be introducing the guest speaker and the story behind the speaker, Ryleigh had Googled and read every article she could find. Although she wanted to be a veterinarian when she grew up, she loved reading Black History. She knew the speaker was very special and wanted to make sure Aniya got all the facts right in introducing her. Ryleigh's teacher arranged to have Aniya's school program live-streamed for the students at Ryleigh's school. But Ryleigh had also arranged to go live on Facebook so the whole world, as Ryleigh put it, would finally get to meet Sarah Collins Rudolph.

"Mom, make Maxwell and Roman give me back my shoes," Aniya yelled. Her brothers had a morning routine of doing whatever they could think of to destroy Aniya's day—or so Aniya thought.

"Boys, give your sister her shoes, and you missy need to get a move-on, or you will be late," her mom warned.

Aniya settled on her "Still I Rise" bow-tie, finished getting dressed and headed out the door. "Bye, mom, remember it starts at 2:00," she shouted as she rushed out the door to catch the school bus.

On the ride to school, Aniya rehearsed in her mind over and over again the lyrics of the song she would sing as part of her introduction. Aniya giggled when thinking about what she would say, because she had to admit that she was using most of the information Ryleigh had researched and sent to her. Aniya also thought about her conversation with her grandmother, whom they called G-von. G-von told Aniya that this speaker and others lived during the Civil Rights Era—a time when Black people were not treated fairly or equally. This speaker and others like her are how Aniya is allowed to attend schools with white youth, live in their neighborhood, and not be limited in life because of segregation. Aniya penciled in a note to remind herself to say thank you to the speaker.

Aniya arrived at school and was greeted by the Principal who was waiting for her bus. *Wow*, she thought, *I have never seen Mr. Blackson in a matching suit.* Like Aniya, Mr. Blackson had also dressed specially for the occasion. It was clear to Aniya he was also very excited, or nervous or both. As they entered the school, Mr. Blackson began to ramble off a to-do list of questions, which reminded Aniya of Ryleigh's repeated calls. Suddenly, her phone buzzed. She carefully looked at her screen so as not to alert Mr. Blackson that she had a phone, or worse yet, that it was on inside the school. It was Ryleigh. Aniya didn't answer the call, and within a second, her phone vibrated, letting her know she now had a text. Yes, it was Ryleigh.

"Make sure when she gives you the autograph, she spells my name correctly: R-y-l-e-i-g-h."

Aniya made her way to her first class, which was History. Her History teacher seemed even more frantic than Mr. Blackson had.

"Aniya, I am glad you arrived early. I have few questions," she said.

"Yes, Ms. Parker, what are they?" Aniya responded, attempting to sound interested.

Ms. Parker shuffled her papers on her desk and said, "Well, where is my list? It was here earlier. Oh, here it is. No, that's not it. OK, here it is."

Aniya felt this was going to be a long day, beginning with this long conversation about to start.

"Aniya, I need you to make sure you emphasize the fact that it was my idea to invite her and to open the program up to the community."

"Yes, Ms. Parker," Aniya responded.

"Then I also need you to remind the audience that I, too, came from Birmingham."

"Yes, Ms. Parker."

As Ms. Parker was attempting to get out her next question, which Aniya realized were not questions but more reminders, like the list Mr. Blackson had discussed with her, a loud group of students arrived. Great, Aniya thought as she found her way to her desk.

It seemed to take forever for 2:00 to come. Aniya was too nervous to eat lunch, so she spent the time in the library going over her introduction and the things she was NOT going to say. In each class, the teacher reminded Aniya of pointers to make. However, none of those pointers had anything to do with the speaker or her story. Aniya decided to stick with the words and format she had worked on all weekend—with the help of her cousin, Ryleigh, of course.

Aniya pulled out her phone to text Ryleigh, "Hey Ry, thank you for the information. We are going to make sure the whole world knows about her."

Seconds later, Ryleigh responded, "I know, Aniya. It's now up to us to learn from her so we can keep her story alive." She paused, and then said, "Hey Aniya, don't mess up."

"Goodbye Ryleigh." Aniya gathered her things and went to her final class before the assembly. She was nervous but excited.

Chapter 2

Virtual Connection

Meanwhile, Ryleigh's school in Biloxi, Mississippi, was getting ready for the virtual presentation of the event that was about to take place at her cousin's school many miles away in Nebraska. When Aniya shared with her family that she had been selected to introduce the speaker and who was coming, the family made a big deal of the occasion. Ryleigh's mom had shared the news with Ryleigh's school and suggested that they also hold a Black History Month All-School Assembly that would connect virtually with the one being held in Nebraska. The Principal agreed, so arrangements were made to have the assembly broadcasted at Ryleigh's school simultaneously.

Ryleigh was excited that her big cousin was introducing the speaker. She was excited that she had been chosen to give a short presentation about the speaker before the virtual broadcast at her own school. Ryleigh wanted to make sure she learned all she could about the speaker.

Much of what she read made her sad. Ryleigh could not believe people could treat other people so badly based on the color of their skin. However, she learned that there were brave people—white and black—who worked together to change the laws that allowed people to be mistreated. She felt even sadder that Ms. Sarah had been left out of most of the history books or articles she had read, but she vowed to work to change that.

Ryleigh was interested in what she read about the Children's Crusade, in which kids her age joined in the marches to end segregation. Over 1,000 kids participated, and some were arrested and jailed. Ryleigh learned that most of their efforts were planned at the same church the speaker attended. Ryleigh wondered if the speaker was part of the Children's Crusade. In doing her research, Ryleigh learned about the Civil Rights Act of 1965 and the Voting Rights Act, which were laws written to make things fair for Black Americans so they could not be denied the rights to eat, shop, play, or attend schools with white people. Ryleigh wondered what she would have done had she lived during the Civil Rights Era.

Chapter 3

The Introduction of Sarah Collins Rudolph

The moment had finally come. It was almost 2:00. The students and teachers had gathered in the school gymnasicafetoriam, a name the students had given to their school's multi-purpose room because it was used as the gymnasium, cafeteria, and auditorium. Members of the community were arriving. Aniya peered from behind the curtain to see if her family was there, and yes, they were front and center. Her papas, grandmothers, parents, auntie, brothers Roman and Maxwell, along with her cousin Brandon were all there.

Aniya felt a soft tap on her shoulder, followed by an even softer voice, "I hear you are the young lady who will be introducing me."

Aniya could not control herself as she suddenly burst into tears. She then felt a strong hand go around her shoulders. "Hi, I am George C. Rudolph, Sarah's husband. Don't cry. Are you nervous? Don't be."

"No," Aniya responded. "I am just so happy to meet her. I want to thank Ms. Sarah; and I am sorry for what happened."

"You are welcome, dear."

Suddenly, Aniya's attention was drawn to Mr. Blackson, who had dropped his note cards on the stage. He was bent over picking them up as he introduced Aniya. The students laughed, and many had snuck out cell phones to video him on his knees trying to pick up the note cards, introduce Aniya, and bring the students to order all at the same time.

Aniya took her place at the microphone.

"I want you, Lord, to walk with me. I want you, Lord, to walk with me. As I travel, sharing my story, I want you, Lord, to walk with me." Aniya had decided to surprise her family and the school with a song as part of her introduction, and had changed some of the words of a Negro Spiritual to fit the occasion. The entire room, including the speaker and her husband, were on their feet clapping and shouting words of encouragement. Aniya introduced the speaker as the audience began to calm down and take their seats, so most people only really heard the part, "Please welcome Sarah Collins Rudolph."

Chapter 4

Addie Mae's Little Sister

"Hello, my name is Sarah Collins Rudolph. I am the little sister of Addie Mae Collins. You might not know her name or mine, but we were the young girls in the basement of the 16th Street Baptist Church on the morning of September 15, 1963, when evil men planted sticks of dynamite under the basement stairs of the church and attached a timer that went off as we were preparing to start our youth program. At the time of the bombing, we were about the same age as most of you. I was 12, my sister Addie Mae, and our friends Cynthia Wesley and Carole Robertson were 14, and Carol Denise McNair, the youngest of us, was 11. My sister and our three friends were killed, but I survived. Yes, I am the fifth little girl who was in the basement that tragic day."

As the speaker continued, her voice began to crack. "A lot of what has been written about that day did not happen as many have said. Like all the other kids there, we were preparing ourselves for the annual youth day at church. My sister Addie Mae and I had walked to church, arriving too late to go to Sunday School. We went down to the ladies' lounge to wait for services. We were later joined by Carol, Cynthia and Denise who went directly to the bathroom stalls, and later joined Addie Mae and me in the lounge area. Like most young girls we were giggling and talking about not much of anything. Denise asked Addie Mae to tie her sash. The last memory I have of my sister was seeing her reach to tie the sash on Denise McNair's dress. Suddenly, the dynamite exploded. I called for Addie Mae, but she didn't answer."

The gymnasicafetoriam had become completely silent. Not a single person moved, and all eyes were on Ms. Sarah.

As Ms. Sarah spoke, some people were dabbing their eyes, including the Mayor and Mr. Blackson. Others had their heads bowed down, but most were frozen in their seats, taking in every word of the brave and courageous speaker. Behind the curtain, George, a Vietnam Veteran, sat with his head down, listening to the story that had become a part of his life too.

George, too, had grown up in segregated Birmingham with Sarah. They attended the same high school but had gone their separate ways after graduation. He remembers the bombing and the years before and after the bombing. He was an eleven-year-old attending church with his parents several blocks away when the bomb went off. He recalls churches all over the city immediately dismissed services and went home. As a child, he had suffered the same fear and treatment that Sarah and other black kids had lived with. He knew of the stories his family and others had experienced because of racism and being treated badly. He, too, had learned to fear things we take for granted, like walking alone, going to school, and even attending church because of the violence that had taken place.

As his wife continued to share her story, George reflected on the months before the church bombing when hundreds of Black youths George's age and younger had participated in the Children's Crusade to bring attention to racism and segregation, especially in the school system. He remembered how water hoses and dogs had been used to attack the young children. He wondered how many had been jailed for days, and reflected on Dr. Martin Luther King Jr.'s visit to the city. George remembered as a young adult how he had left to serve in the military and was sent to Vietnam to fight for the rights of others, while back home, Black Americans like him did not fully have these rights. George looked up because he knew his wife had reached the part in her speech about being hospitalized and blinded by the blast. This was the hardest part of the story to hear.

"Because of my injuries," Ms. Sarah continued with her voice trembling, "I was not able to attend my sister's funeral, which hurts me to this day because Addie Mae and I were very close. I loved my sister, but I was in the hospital with glass bits still in my body. It was many years later before they were able to remove all of them. At first, I was blinded in both eyes, but the vision in my left eye returned, but I still wear a false eye because I was not able to get the vision back in my right eye. Not only did I lose my sister that day, but I lost any hope of becoming a nurse, which is what I wanted to be. I have always wanted to help people.

"Even though I had lost my eyesight because of hate, being blinded by hate gave me the chance to see what hate can do if you allow it to take over. This is why I have chosen a life of love. I don't hate the men who planted the bomb. I have forgiven them, and that is what we all must do. Learn the power of love and forgiveness." The audience applauded and then settled down to let her continue.

Ms. Sarah explained that during the Civil Rights Era she grew up in, her city had so much hatred toward Black people that it was nicknamed

Bombingham. Three bombs had been set off in the days before the church bombing to harass and intimidate Black people. However, this was the first time a bomb had been placed inside a church to kill people. Before the bombing, the federal government had ordered the integration of public schools in Alabama. Ms. Sarah explained that many people felt her church was chosen because it had been used by Civil Rights advocates like Dr. Martin Luther King Jr. to plan the marches—including the Children's Crusade, which demanded integration.

Ms. Sarah also explained that most of the stories written about the church bombing not only leave her out and distort what the girls were doing moments before the bombing, but until recently, have left out the two other children killed that day. "We must honor their names too."

She paused for a moment, and continued, "After the bombing, chaos broke out in the city. The Black community had had enough. The bombing of the Church was more than most could take."

"Unbeknownst to 13-year-old Virgil Ware, the bombing had occurred and demonstrations had broken out by Blacks and anti-Civil Rights Whites throughout Birmingham. Virgil and his brother were riding bikes when they encountered two white boys who fired several gunshots at them, striking Virgil in the cheek and chest, and killing him on the spot."

Sarah continued, "Across town later that day, a group of Black boys were confronted by a carload of white boys who drove by throwing bottles and rocks. Johnny Robinson, age 16, was among the group of Black teens. He threw a rock back as the police were called to the area. Johnny ran away and was struck in the back of the head by police gunfire, killing him instantly. Like my name, Sarah Collins Rudolph, the names of these two additional victims from that day are rarely mentioned. It is as if History has been purposefully altered to forget about us."

Chapter 5

The Children's Crusade

Ms. Sarah was not part of the Children's Crusade, but knew kids who did participate. As Ms. Sarah explained to the audience, "The Children's Crusade took place May 2, 1963, just 4 months before the church bombing. Neither I nor Addie Mae, nor the other girls participated. Some of our parents might have been involved in helping to organize it, but none of us girls were involved." As she continued, "On May 2nd, thousands of kids left school to gather at the 16th Street Baptist Church. On the news that night, the world saw how the kids were attacked. The governor and police commissioner ordered high-powered hoses that had enough force to rip the bark off a tree, and German Shepherd dogs to be used on the kids. These were just babies trying to make things right for us."

Sarah continued, as she looked at the faces in the audience, "One of the girls arrested was Audrey Faye Hendricks who was just 8 years old. She was considered the youngest person to be arrested along with 500 other kids, some of whom spent nearly a week in jail, along with Dr. King and other adults who joined in the protest. In fact, it was while Dr. King was jailed that he wrote one of his many famous letters. Dr. King told the youth that what they were doing would impact Black kids in the future.

"Well, the march was a success," Ms. Sarah continued. "People did not like how the children had been treated. Their cries for justice forced the President of the United States to get laws passed to end segregation. Within a few months of the march, President Kennedy said he would be introducing new Civil Rights Legislation. Some people in Birmingham grew even more angry, and might have lead to the bombing at our Church. I don't know for sure, but I believe it is so."

Ms. Sarah's voice trailed off into nearly a whisper. She took a drink of water and continued, "Later that same year, President Kennedy was assassinated, and President Johnson, the next President, got the laws passes promised by President Kennedy."

Chapter 6

The Civil Rights Era

Aniya, like the rest of the audience, clung to every word from Ms. Sarah's mouth, and these stories sounded familiar from the research she and Ryleigh had done. She also remembered the stories from hanging out in Mama's Attic, a humanities center started by her grandmother G-Von to share the stories of Black people. Aniya recalled that based on her research Dr. King had just given his famous I Have A Dream speech to an audience of over 250,000 people in Washington D.C., on August 28, 1963, right before the bombing. She also remembered stories that around the country, young people rose up to advance the Civil Rights Movement and end segregation.

Ms. Sarah reminded the young people in the room that they each carry the torch of justice for future generations. She reminded them of the impact young people have made in advancing Civil Rights and social justice, and she provided a timeline of actions young people had taken before the Church bombing.

"Three years before the famous March on Washington, 17-year-old Franklin McCain and three of his friends, Ezell Blair, Jr., Joseph A. McNeil, and David Richmond sought to integrate the lunch counter at a Woolworth's store in Greensboro, North Carolina. Remember their names," pleaded Ms. Sarah. "Children such as Ruby Bridges, who at age 6 was the first to integrate a public school in the South in 1960, after Vicki Henderson, Donald Henderson, Linda Brown, James Emanuel, Nancy Todd, Katherine Carper the child-plaintiffs in Brown vs. Board of Education made it possible by bringing a legal challenge in 1954 to separate-but-equal laws in education. You must remember their names."

Sarah continued to speak, and the audience remained silent and still, "Many of you do not know that Claudette Colvin was arrested at the age of 15 in Montgomery, Alabama, for refusing to give up her seat to a white woman on a crowded, segregated bus on March 2, 1955, nine months before Rosa Parks did the same. Claudette became one of the four plaintiffs to fight bus segregation through the United States court system in Alabama and won. Minnijean Brown, Elizabeth Eckford, Ernest

Green, Thelma Mothershed, Melba Patillo, Gloria Ray, Terrence Roberts, Jefferson Thomas and Carolotta Walls were the nine students who made up the Little Rock Nine who became known for the violence they endured in efforts to integrate Central High School in Little Rock, Arkansas, two years after Brown vs. Board of Education had outlawed school segregation. There were so many efforts made by young people to change the laws, but you must not just teach or learn about the historical moments, you must also learn and remember their names," she said as she renewed her plea to the audience.

"Yes, there were numerous efforts by young people to bring about changes in laws permitting the separation of Blacks and Whites, but the mistreatment of the children during the Children's Crusade, followed by the Church bombing that killed Addie Mae Collins, Denise McNair, Cynthia Wesley and Carole Robertson, and severely injuring Sarah Collins were by far the incidents having the greatest impact in dismantling America's wall of segregation and advancing Civil Rights.

After the Church bombing, three major civil rights laws were passed—the Civil Rights Act of 1964, The Voting Rights Act of 1965, and the Fair Housing Act of 1968.

While the war on segregation ended for Black Americans with the passage of Civil Rights laws, the battle was just beginning for young Sarah Collins, the only survivor in the basement when the dynamite went off. Her small body was rippled with shards of glass, including pieces that lodged in her face causing blindness in both eyes. She eventually regained sight in her left eye. Sarah spent two months in the hospital recovering from her injuries. Her 12-year-old body, ravaged with glass shards and debris from the bombing, would never be the same. No law passed in the months and years following the bomb could make it better for little Sarah.

Chapter 7

Call to Action

As Ms. Sarah was winding up her remarks, her voice got stronger and louder, " Boys, girls, parents, and teachers: Each of you have a duty to make sure our History is complete and accurate. You have a duty to make sure historical moments are not forgotten regardless of how painful." Ms. Sarah told the audience. "Each day when I wake up," she continued, " I am reminded of one of the worst periods in our country's History. I have to live each day with the mental and physical scars from September 15, 1963. There is not one day that I do not think about my sister and what she would have become. Not one day passes that I do not think about my dream of being a nurse, but I do not let this stop me." She stepped from the podium and walked into the audience, "I am the fifth little girl that America was never told about, and I feel I was spared to not only make sure the story is told correctly, but as a reminder of what can happen when hate is allowed to take over. I am Sarah Collins Rudolph, the little sister to Addie Mae Collins, and this is my story."

The audience stood and applauded for a long time as she looked at the faces staring back at her. She stepped down from the stage and walked through the audience hugging kids and adults who had gathered.

As Ms. Sarah made her way through the audience, kids who forgot about the school's no-phone policy were taking selfies. So were adults who had come to hear and finally meet Ms. Sarah Collins Rudolph, the fifth little girl in the Church bombing.

Mr. Blackson was attempting to call for order, but like most assemblies, no one was listening. Aniya was making her way to her family when her phone went off. Before even looking to see who it was, she said, "Ryleigh, this was awesome. We got to meet History."

"Oh, Aniya, you are so lucky to have met her in person, but our school loved her story, too. We hope to bring her to our school one day. Can you ask her to come? Aniya, let me speak to her, please."

"I can't let you speak to her Ry; there are millions of people around her," Aniya said with a slight exaggeration.

Just as Aniya was completing her sentence, Mr. George, who was standing right behind her, reached for her phone and said, "I can help you. Aniya. Who is on the phone?"

"It's my cousin, Ryleigh, who lives in Biloxi. She helped me with the introduction."

Mr. George waved to his wife to get her attention. "Sarah, I have Ryleigh in Biloxi on the phone, and she wants to speak with you."

***

Later that evening Ryleigh and Aniya talked about all they had experienced and what they planned to do to make sure they continue this story for Ms. Sarah. They decided they were going to suggest that the next family vacation take place in Birmingham, and what they were going to do to learn more about Civil Rights and Ms. Sarah's story.

"Well I have a book report, and I am going to change my book to one on Ms. Sarah Collins Rudolph," said Ryleigh.

"Good luck," Aniya said, almost as much a warning as a wish. "Remember I could not find any books on her, but that's going to change after today. I am going to form a Sarah Collins Rudolph History Club. Email and tweet to every newspaper, tv station, and all the important people like the mayor, governors, senators, and celebrities to tell them about her.

"Oh, Aniya, that's a good idea. Can I be a member of the Club? I can use my technology skills to build our website, and Facebook page, and we can have a Club in Nebraska and Mississippi, and I can get my grandparents in Ohio to start one, too."

The girls swapped ideas back and forth texting and talking until both moms took their phones.

After a year of planning, the History club became a reality and was named the Sarah Collins Rudolph History Club. Mrs. Sarah returned for the ribbon cutting. The purpose of the Club is to teach young people about the role young people played in changing our world and to make sure the names of the young people are remembered.

Sarah and George continue to travel the world sharing her story, helping correct the historical accounts of that day, and teaching about the Civil Rights Movement.

www.ingramcontent.com/pod-product-compliance
Lightning Source LLC
Chambersburg PA
CBHW040758150426
42811CB00055B/1018